don't call me a
TART

recipes by elizabeth beekley & cecelia korn
photography by bitna chung

dedicated to each and every butter, sugar, and flour-obsessed member of

evelyn carrion · veronica martin · amy milbauer · jeff willis + joseph tonn · tashia · ivan beekley · rachel prickett · edward f
kinkade · whitney burnside · rebecca mischel · andy olshin · scott dolich · merideth andrews · tess beekley · timo daily · trev
acker · barb foulk · marven winters · becky rainbow · rick steffan · penny hanselman · joan korn · andrea bonard · courtney
munch · jerri breene · camille stark · debbie webster · vicki pelich · emily griffith · armain austin · delona lang · lawrence rei
· nancy chafin · alissa cattone · katie perko · calvin young · juliann e bailey · jean lo · steve prosser · kevin burnett · dana re
anne warner · linda cline · kristy anderson · wendy copeland · joe volpert · shobha ramprasad · briana schellhaas · michelle
manning · paula wynn · teresa campbell · gina fleschner · linda greenman · lori lassere-gullion · melanie atkinson · kathy p
melissa collier · kelley dougherty · vicki wong · emily whitney · joyce m howard · asha petoskey · cinamon miller · justin mi
cheri peden · ron miller · anne nisbet · claire lewis · carly warner · caren smeltzer · evanna c koska · lynn buechler · shari kat
· allison victor · brenda withycombe · sherry. stricker · linda leigh paul · andrew self · heather endicott · jeanne franzoni · lo
angela k burnett · ruby wynn · desiree bliss · robin peterson · nicholas peterka · patricia glennon · sarah dougher · catherine
christine huang · christine deladisma · colleen johnson · traci liu
morgan · tricia juettemeyer · sarah oliver · kari thomas · corinna casey · mel lee · nicole wong · olga rosas · mary lou dougla
elshamy · suzy pak · janet stearns-gannett · larry mcdonald · valerie stallings · porche lovely · jm walters · karla kaudel · robin
ross · rebecca sachs · gina leon · randall goodman · barb harold · jennifer griffin-valeri · naomi tsurum
korman · tiffany yee · erika dyer · barbara fisher · karen miller · jeanne decker · aurora morgan · paul gossinger · chamren ho
swope · tiffany tipps · stefanie howard · chelsea ellavsky · katherine wax · michael cassella · victoria l wetle · yonette fine · m
· margaret smith · jacob dyer · juliana mar · jennifer gonzalez birk · robin owens · karla mcgee · kay cuningham · diann osterlu
j servera · acorn marketing · katie breene · efsun kayi · kara reynolds · traci morgan · sam jacks · dan fredma
gill · ara vallaster · douglas griffith · rick peterson · personal · suzy pak · mary hoeflich · sophie acker · elizabeth warren · ter
teri lund · kathleen nagavi · jon + paula lebre · claire harrison · kendra key · britney hardie · theresa sleight · adrienne martin
o'brien · teri tremblay · gary driggs · melissa collier · pieter rowlette · laurel pickett · lynn adamo · marilyn kakudo · cary pe
brandt · carol sherar · howard kinkade · debbie webster · pat kaplan · youlee you · josh hodsden · brent norman · alison +
moser · kara reynolds · fawn mcgee · jon + paula lebre · rosemary suttle · amanda collier · marilyn's sweet dad · nanny + po
waldron · kevin burnett · dana reames · heidi kaplan · michelle lung · brenda sparks · kathy perko · patricia selby · justin mi
· colleen johnson · dana fitzgerald · jennifer gifford · carol briney · jamie june · traci liu · terri kirby · corinna casey · mel lee
jennifer griffin-valeri · naomi tsurumi · kathryn conway · michelle tubbs · adrienne baghdadi · barbara gleasman · barbara
horn · kris moore + ryan wilcoxen · karen gleason · gillian johnston · tricia greco · allison chang · michelle mcguire · yonette
gonzalez birk · robin owens · karla mcgee · kay cuningham · diann osterlund · barb foulke · efsun kayi · renee yoon · jolie kre
pickett · lynn adamo · marilyn kakudo · cary perkins · eileen winters · alison + andrew gold · anandhi celeste · bella beekley
olga rosas · julia guthrie · barbara shleifer · susan slater · irene sheppard · yonette fine · manny veloso · meagan porter · val
gipson · avery quinn · mila gabriel · yonette fine · manny veloso · valerie o'brien · nick robinson · the korn sisters · cecelia ha

le fudge · juli bailey · marcus lintner · julia guthrie · martha holmberg· kara reynolds · cory schreiber · dan beekley · holly

matthew weatherman · jessica noyes · nicki passarella · amber holland· sharon hennessy · may low · mary kay korn ·sophie

rchert · rosemary petty · jeannie johnson ·monica garcia + veronica portilla · carol nelson · patricia l souza · annie + ernie

racey waldron · cheryl pulliam · robin budde · grasso greg · laura greenberg · hannah ferber · marcella barker · cheri peden

eidi kaplan · andré schellhaas · allison victor · eric joyner · marsha miller · violet zuzu vega · susan tardif · olivia finn vega ·

nda sparks · sabine e welling · elise kirkpatrick · vicki bye · vicki wong · kristin hakala · mora chartrand · carol greiwe · peter

tricia selby · jeff stallard · kathryn schmidt · kate o'neill · patricia rimmer · rachel prickett · janet bakes · pamela wilkinson ·

ura potter · linda m massey · carol briney · elizabeth rutledge-shryock · katherine mccollam · byron coulter · shiva nayeri

simmons · bonnie berg · barb marold · sahra rahimtoola · rebecca j singer · april haddock · tracey vannevele · virginia david

oto · fumi rohman · renee hartig · robin sippel · danita d melott · shannan shute · ann jones · molly docherty · kathy stitt ·

ler · kelly witty · yuridia mcgaha · lynn gillison-acorn marketing · kim cutsforth · jaclyn godic · deborah thomas · rob coury ·

y hathaway · john briggs · kristina kochel · cheryl lawson · sara javoronok · pam martin · kara reynolds · sara gielow · diane

eth carney halladay · susan smallsreed · joan carney · mary humphreys · hateful heather hanselman · joanne mikol · hoda

denise alonso · mark smith · carrie owens · joseph tonn · jerri breene · valerie o'brien · louise baxter · alyssa vasquez · rebecca

n conway · elle os · a r add arbra gle n hle s ter rene sheppard · laura

moore + ryan ilco ren an an tri co ison a mi ell rue · susan ko · caroline

oso · meagan ort a it nne ann nd en eath he la el s ab n ann · betsy wahlquist

b foulke · jennifer crowley · david g volke · darcy martin · tara garcia · maria bruce · grayson dempsey · cynthia kraft · carlos

ha williams · jennifer rogers · nathan hostler · paul lopez · janet young · leanna mackenzie · bernadette zaharchook · janette

rts · amy jarvis · megan mcbride · merris sumrall · jan priddy · katie lyons · lynette child · elizabeth bodenner · kelsey priest

esch · deborah pack-patton · joan thompson · supattra namnon · marianne krainock · linnea gilson · mary k korn · michelle

een winters · rande degidio · sari jouihan · kim dang · deborah mandell · harry peterson-nedry · amy jarvis · james + becky

gold · anandhi celeste · john long · sue moore · lynne + michael madigan · dan beekley · mary nelson · kristin paul · susan

eekley · kathy smith · edward f korn · nicole fudge · courtney anne borchert · rosemary petty · lawrence reichman · tracey

aura potter · shari katz · renee simmons · jeanne franzoni · lori hokomoto · fumi rohman · catherine ann miller · kelly witty

wong · olga rosas · mary lou douglas · elizabeth carney halladay · randall goodman · barb marold · laurabeth ragozzino ·

· susan slater · irene sheppard · barbra fisher · karen miller · jeanne decker · aurora morgan · paul schlesinger · chamren

nny veloso · meagan porter · marlee smith-janney · ann andersen · heather heck · laurel slatt · elizabeth haimann · jennifer

· valerie o'brien · dana sacks · dan fredman · marsha williams · adrianne martin · leila mesch · deborah pack-patton · laurel

e · fat mike ·michele kinkade nanny + pop-pop beekley · kathy smith · justin mitchell · laura potter · mel lee · nicole wong ·

en · hazel sacks · ara vallaster · dana sacks · duane inglish · dorie mellon · sue pearcy-gonzales · gayle inglish gipson · grace

a knoblach · sweet · ivan beekley · martha holmberg · sharon grazel · evie babbie · tess beekley · the dang sisters · may low

TARTNATION

I have a confession to make.

I never, ever read the pages of a cookbook that precede the actual recipes.

Nope. I'm too excited to get right down to the baking part of things - the "let's get our hands, kitchen, and clothing completely covered with flour" piece of the action. Yes, I am impatient. Yes, I am fired up and eager to get started. But after ten years of commercial baking, I might ask some forgiveness in flipping past those initial pages.

If you feel confident in your abilities, then skip right on by the sermon on ingredients, scales, and such. However, if you purchased this book because you absolutely need to be able to recreate your favorite Two Tarts cookie and perfect it down to the last crumb, then you'll want to reference the following pages.

great ingredients
make awesome cookies

BUTTER

In the U.S., salted butter is generally made from older cream. Salt acts as a preservative, extending the shelf life and masking the actual freshness of the butter. For best results, choose unsalted butter. This allows *you* to be in charge of the amount of salt in the recipe. It also allows you to choose a quality salt.

WHAT TO LOOK FOR

1. Seek out fresh, unsalted butter produced by a local dairy or farmers' co-op.

2. The ingredient list should contain one, and only one ingredient: cream.

3. Avoid house brands. These are created to provide extra margin for the grocer, not because they are on a mission to provide you with the best flavor profile.

4. European-style butters, while lovely and decadent, have a higher percentage of butterfat than standard butters, and will result in a different texture.

EGGS

Remember when eggs at the grocery store were sold at room temperature? Unwashed eggs are covered by a natural cuticle that keeps the egg fresh and prevents most bacteria from penetrating the shell. Today, the USDA requires that all eggs be washed before sale, effectively removing the natural, protective cuticle. That's why the eggs at your local market are now stored in the refrigerator section.

WHAT TO LOOK FOR

1. Fresh, organic, pasture-raised eggs from a local farmers' market or co-op

2. "Cage-free" eggs are not necessarily of high quality. Don't be fooled: cage-free eggs are not the same as "pasture-raised."

3. Check dates. Fresh eggs not only taste better, but will perform better in recipes. Whites should be thick and gelatinous - this is the sign of a truly fresh egg.

FLOUR

Commercially-milled flours are made from two types of wheat. Winter wheat, known as "hard wheat," has a higher protein content that is appropriate for making bread and pasta. For pastry, we look for "soft wheat" flours, sown in spring and harvested in fall. Flours made from spring wheat, such as pastry flour, yield more tender baked goods.

WHAT TO LOOK FOR

1. Small bags of unbleached, low-gluten, wheat flour (not whole wheat)

2. Flours labeled as "pastry flour" are lowest in protein content, but all-purpose flour is an acceptable replacement for pastry flour.

3. Purchase only the amount of flour you need for each baking project. Flour goes rancid quickly, but you might not notice (who the heck sticks their finger into a bag of flour to taste it?)

MILK AND CREAM

A truly fresh glass of milk can be magical. Our dad, who grew up on a dairy farm, said that milk quality is dependent on the breed of cow producing it. The Holstein is the most common dairy breed in the U.S., producing large amounts of so-so milk with very little cream or protein content. Jerseys and Guernseys, on the other hand, yield smaller quantities of richer, more flavorful milk. If you are lucky enough to have a local dairy nearby, find out what type of cows they keep!

WHAT TO LOOK FOR

1. Whole, organic milk from a local dairy or co-op

2. Heavy cream with a fat content of 36-40%

3. Avoid "ultra pasturized" milk and cream. Excessive pasturization destroys milk sugars, resulting in a flavorless dairy product with a suspiciously long shelf life.

NUTS

Ever taste a stale, or worse yet, a rancid nut? Nasty. Who wants to bite into a hazelnut baci made with old nuts? No thanks. Buy small quantities of fresh nuts. Keep them in an air-tight container, and store them in the fridge. The day before you plan to bake with them, toast them in the oven to remove excess moisture and brighten the flavor of the nuts.

WHAT TO LOOK FOR

1. Raw or recently roasted nuts from a small, local grower

2. Nuts are seasonal - ask the farmer when they were harvested. A good grower will keep the nuts in shell until just before they are sold. Shell-on nuts kept in cool storage will stay fresh for a year or more.

3. Taste before you buy, especially if you are purchasing nuts from a bulk bin.

SALT

It doesn't seem like much, that pinch of salt, but good, flavorful salt of proper consistency can make or break a recipe. Skip the Kosher salt - the wide flake will not integrate into the doughs evenly, and it doesn't taste any better than the bleached table salts that have been stripped of their minerals (which are then, ironically, sold to manufacturers of vitamin supplements). Oh, and that ubiquitous table salt up in your cupboard? Chances are it contains additives such as talc, ferrocyanide, and silica aluminate. Who would eat this stuff?

WHAT TO LOOK FOR

1. Unbleached, fine-grained sea salt

2. Finishing salt, while amazing on top of a fleur-de-sel chocolate chip cookie, is best suited to actual finishing purposes. The special crystalline structure isn't ideal for widespread use in doughs. Plus, finishing salts tend to be wallet-rippingly expensive, so save them for special uses.

cheap
ingredients
rarely taste
good

Bakers are a rather particular lot.

And that's putting it kindly.

If you've ignored our confession and already skipped ahead, you might be wondering why on Earth we've placed the gram conversions first and foremost, with standard measurements relegated to parenthesis. To tell the truth, it goes against a baker's grain to include standard measurements at all. Weights are more accurate than measurements. That's why commercial bakers read recipes by weight. Think we're being a little Type A? Well, we are - but for good reason. We are not line cooks. Line cooks have the flexibility to add a little more seasoning here, or a splash of something or other there. A baker's primary concern is to produce a consistent product. And standard measurements in no way allow us to do that. Ounces and grams, however, lead to perfection.

Consider a simple cup of flour. To measure that flour, you might have dragged the measuring cup through the bag or cannister, leveled it off, and considered it good. But didn't you just compact that flour as you dragged it through the bag? It now weighs more than an "average" cup of flour. What if you were down to the last of your flour, and opted to pour it into that same cup measure? In doing so, you inadvertently sifted it, causing the flour to weigh slightly less than the "average" cup. Is your cup measure one of those stainless steel jobs, dinged and dented from years of use? Those dents will cause your measurements to be off as well. If perfection in baking is not your thing, then by all means, bake by measurement. But if you are puzzled as to why you can't consistently reproduce your favorite baked goods, we have a cure.

Buy a scale.

Any digital scale will do. Cheap ones run $30-$40 and will last several years. Then, and only then, will you be able to recreate these recipes the way they were intended. Rather than guessing what a "scant ⅓ cup" looks like, you can weigh your ingredients to the gram. Your inner engineer will thank you.

your
new
bff

Everyone knows how to make drop cookies.

Easy, right?

But here's where things can get a little weird. See, everyone who has ever baked a snickerdoodle or a chocolate chip cookie has a predetermined texture in mind. Drop cookies are the Myers-Briggs Test of the baking world, the psychoanalytic school of texture. So let's do some Ph.D. work.

Ask your friends how they like their chocolate chip cookie. We guarantee you will not get a shrug and a quizzical look. Instead, you'll hear something like, "crunchy around the edges, but soft and a little chewy inside." Or maybe your friend is a "thin and snappy" kind of person. How about a "gooey and underdone?" We once had a customer who liked cookies that were, in our opinion, overbaked. Rather than composting them, we saved them for her. In time, they became known as "Merris cookies."

I think we're tapping into some basic childhood memories here. Like music, food has that magical ability to transport us back to a very specific time and place. At 90, our dad no longer remembered who we were, but he could still wax poetic about our grandmother's spice cookies.

So how do these recipes rate? Well, our DCMPI (drop cookie maximum perfection index) hovers around "puffy and chewy." We like our cookies slightly soft, with a tiny bit of crunch in the shell portion. If you prefer your cookies on the crispy side, keep them in the oven a minute longer. Like them undercooked? You know what to do.

Leavening plays an important part in all of this. Baking soda causes more of the spreading, crisping, and browning phenomenon, while baking powder yields cookies that are puffy and lighter in color. We encourage you to play around with the leavening in tiny increments. Find your perfect DCMPI!

chocolate chip
fleur-de-sel
makes 48 cookies

Here it is - our most firetruckin' popular cookie ever. When we first began sprinkling our chocolate chip cookies with finishing salt, folks looked at us as though we had lost our minds. A year later, The NY Times published a similar recipe, and suddenly, we weren't (as) crazy. Hey, whatever gets you to put these in your mouth! Remember, a little finishing salt goes a long way, so use sparingly.

224 g (1 c) unsalted butter, softened
150 g (¾ c) granulated sugar
94 g (2 large) eggs
5 g (1 t) baking soda
280 g (10 oz) dark chocolate pistoles or chips

150 g (¾ c) light brown muscovado sugar
5 g (1 t) good quality vanilla extract
364 g (2½ c) low-gluten flour
5 g (1 t) fine sea salt

for finishing:

2 T Fleur-de-sel or other finishing salt (we like fleur-de-sel from Isle de Noirmoutier)

In the bowl of a stand mixer fitted with a paddle attachment, cream the butter, sugars, and vanilla extract until light and fluffy, about 3-4 minutes. Add the eggs one at a time, beating for one minute between additions. In a separate bowl, stir together the flour, baking soda, and fine-grained sea salt (NOT the finishing salt.) With mixer on low, add the dry ingredients, mixing gently until just incorporated. Stop the mixer, scrape down the sides of the bowl, and continue to beat on low for another 30 seconds. Using a spatula or a wooden spoon, fold in the chocolate by hand. Transfer dough to an airtight container and refrigerate overnight. (This is very important - if you bake the cookies when the dough is soft, it will affect the shape and texture.)

Preheat oven to 350° F. Line two baking sheets with parchment paper. Using a #80 scoop, shape the cookies into half-rounds. Arrange cookies 2" apart on the baking sheets, staggering each row. Bake until the cookies are just beginning to set - about 8-10 minutes. Remove tray from the oven and sprinkle each cookie with a few grains of finishing salt. Return tray to the oven and continue to bake until pale golden. (Keep in mind that the cookies will continue to brown as they cool.) Remove from oven. Slide parchment from tray and onto countertop. Cool at least long enough that they won't burn the roof of your mouth. Store at room temperature in an airtight container for up to four days.

sugardoodles

makes 48 cookies

Loyal to their sweet sugar core, snickerdoodle fans are as rabid as they come. For these devotées, no other cookie will do. As suggested by the title of this recipe, our snickerdoodle recipe doubles as a sugar cookie - just skip the cinnamon! While most snickerdoodle recipes contain cream of tartar, ours does not. The resulting cookie is a deeply satisfying, chewy-crispy bite of buttery goodness.

224 g (1 c) unsalted butter, softened
5 g (1 t) good quality vanilla extract
336 g (2⅓ c) low-gluten flour
2 g (½ t) baking powder

294 g (1½ c) granulated sugar
47 g (1 large) whole egg
5 g (1 t) baking soda
2 g (½ t) fine sea salt

for finishing:

112 g (½ c) granulated sugar + 1 T ground cinnamon   *or*   112 g (½ c) raw sugar

In the bowl of a stand mixer fitted with a paddle attachment, cream the butter, sugar, and vanilla extract until light and fluffy, about 3-4 minutes. Add the egg and continue to beat until smooth, about two minutes. In a separate bowl, stir together the flour, baking soda, baking powder, and salt. With mixer on low, add the dry ingredients, mixing gently until just incorporated. Stop the mixer, scrape down the sides of the bowl, and continue to beat on low for another 30 seconds. Transfer dough to an airtight container and refrigerate until firm, at least two hours.

Preheat oven to 350° F. Line two baking sheets with parchment paper. Using a #80 scoop, shape the cookies into half-rounds. Moisten your hands with a bit of cold water. Roll each scoop of dough Into a ball. Dredge in your choice of raw sugar (for sugar cookies) or cinnamon sugar (for snickerdoodles). Arrange cookies 2" apart on the baking sheets, staggering each row. Bake until the cookies are just barely beginning to crackle on top and color at the edges, about 8-10 minutes. If you prefer your cookies crispy rather than chewy, bake an additional 1-2 minutes, or until the cookies begin to deflate. Remove from oven. Slide parchment from tray and cool to room temperature. Store in an airtight container at room temperature for up to five days.

ginger molasses chews

makes 48 cookies

It's hard to pick a favorite cookie. During the warmer months, brighter, fruit-filled cookies capture our heart and rule our mixing bowls. But when leaves begin to color and fall, we are lulled on back to the homespun, fragrant, spice-based varieties. These chewy, triple ginger cookies are just the ticket for that first nippy day of fall. If you are not a fan of ginger, you might want to skip right on over these.

168 g (12 T) unsalted butter
196 g (1 c) granulated sugar
47 g (1 large) egg
3 g (½ t) baking soda
3 g (½ t) ground clove
6 g (1½ t) ground ginger

70 g (⅓ c) blackstrap molasses
15 g (2 T) fresh ginger, peeled and grated
245 g (1¾ c) low-gluten flour
2 g (½ t) fine sea salt
6 g (1½ t) ground Saigon cinnamon
84 g (⅓ c) candied ginger, finely diced

In a small, stainless steel saucepan, warm the butter until melted. Place the sugar, molasses, and grated ginger in the bowl of a stand mixer fitted with a paddle attachment. Add the melted butter. Mix at medium speed until combined, 1-2 minutes. Add the egg and mix one more minute. In a separate bowl, stir together all remaining ingredients. With mixer on low, add the dry ingredients, mixing gently until just incorporated. Stop the mixer, scrape down the sides of the bowl, and continue to beat on low for another 30 seconds. Transfer dough to an airtight container and refrigerate at least 2 hours, or until firm.

Preheat oven to 350° F. Line two baking sheets with parchment paper. Using a #80 scoop, shape the dough into half-rounds. Arrange cookies 2" apart on the baking sheets, staggering each row. Bake until the cookies are beginning to color at the edges, tops are set and crinkles begin to form, about 8-10 minutes. This will yield a chewy, soft cookie. (If you prefer more of a ginger "snap," continue to bake another minute or two, until the cookies begin to deflate.) Remove from oven. Slide parchment from tray and cool to room temperature. Store in an airtight container at room temperature for up to one week.

ANZAC biscuits

makes 36 cookies

At some point in her late 20s, Cecelia took a job in Wellington, New Zealand. It sounded so exotic compared to the large farm town in which we grew up. We could only imagine how lush, green, wooly, and windy it must be. During one of her yearly visits home, Cecelia introduced us to her new friend, the ANZAC biscuit, Australia and New Zealand's beloved national cookie. A special golden syrup (available in the syrup aisle of most grocery stores) gives these coconut oatmeal cookies a crunchy, chewy, otherworldly texture.

140 g (1 c) low-gluten flour
84 g (1 c) chipped coconut (thick flakes)
5 g (1 t) baking powder
42 g (¼ c) Lyle's Golden Syrup

105 g (1 c) thick rolled oats
5 g (1 t) baking soda
142 g (10 T) unsalted butter
133 g (⅔ c) granulated sugar

Preheat oven to 350° F. Line two baking sheets with parchment paper. In a large mixing bowl, stir together the flour, oats, coconut flakes, baking soda, and baking powder. Set aside the dry ingredients. In a small, stainless steel saucepan, melt the butter. Add the golden syrup and sugar. Cook, stirring occasionally, over medium heat until the sugar is dissolved and the mixture begins to bubble uniformly. Pour the hot syrup over the dry ingredients. Using a wooden spoon, quickly stir the syrup into the oat mixture until a cohesive dough is formed. (It will be rather buttery and hot.)

Using a #80 scoop, shape the cookies into half-rounds. The dough will be hot, so take care with your fingers! Arrange cookies 2" apart on the baking sheets, staggering each row. Bake until the cookies are light golden in color - about 8-10 minutes. Remove tray from the oven and quickly flatten each cookie with the back of a metal measuring cup. Return tray to the oven and continue to bake until golden throughout. Remove from oven. Slide parchment from tray and allow to cool. The biscuits will become crispy as they cool. Store at room temperature in an airtight container for up to one week.

honey currant oatmeal

makes 48 cookies

Oatmeal. The sleeper cookie. Nothing smells better than a tray of oatmeal cookies cooling on your counter-top. So what if they're not fancy? These golden, puffy, chewy oatmeal cookies are studded with dried black currants and orange zest. Real currants are best, but Zante currants (really just tiny raisins) will do in a pinch. Use old fashioned, thick cut oats for a super chewy cookie.

224 g (1 c) unsalted butter, softened
56 g (⅓ c) raw, local honey
finely grated zest of one small orange
224 g (2½ c) thick, rolled oats
2 g (⅓ t) fine sea salt
126 g (1 c) dried black currants

150 g (¾ c) granulated sugar
14 g (1 T) good quality vanilla extract
176 g (1¼ c) low-gluten flour
4 g (¾ t) baking soda
3 g (1 t) ground Saigon cinnamon

In the bowl of a stand mixer fitted with a paddle attachment, cream the butter, sugar, honey, vanilla extract, and orange zest until light and fluffy, about 3-4 minutes. In a separate bowl, stir together the flour, oats, baking soda, cinnamon, salt, and currants. With mixer on low, add the dry ingredients, mixing gently until just incorporated. Stop the mixer, scrape down the sides of the bowl, and continue to beat on low for another 30 seconds. Transfer dough to an airtight container and refrigerate for at least one hour.

Preheat oven to 350° F. Line two baking sheets with parchment paper. Using a #80 scoop, shape the cookies into half-rounds. Arrange cookies 2" apart on the baking sheets, staggering each row. Place in preheated oven. After 8-9 minutes, when cookies are beginning to color, remove tray from the oven. Gently flatten each cookie by tapping with the bottom of a metal measuring cup. Return to the oven and bake until evenly golden in color, another 2-3 minutes. Slide parchment from tray and cool. Store in a tightly sealed container at room temperature for up to one week.

double chocolate chews

makes 24 cookies

If you're wild about chocolate, why go half way? Here's a super fudgy, dark chocolate cookie studded with a second helping of bittersweet chocolate. Warm from the oven, these are sure to make your day. (Or week, depending on how it's shaping up!) These cookies are best eaten within a day or two of baking, which really isn't an issue in most households. Be sure to use a chocolate with 60% cocoa mass for the dough. Substituting a chocolate with higher or lower cocoa mass will change the ratio of sugar to fat, resulting in an entirely different texture.

28 g (2 T) unsalted butter
94 g (2 large) eggs
59 g (⅓ c) light brown sugar
36g (3 T) low-gluten flour
168 g (6 oz) dark chocolate (60-70%) chopped into small chunks

168 g (6 oz) 60% chocolate, finely chopped
59 g (⅓ c) granulated sugar
5 g (1 t) good quality vanilla extract
1 g (¼ t) baking powder

In a small, stainless steel saucepan, melt the butter over medium heat. Remove from heat. Add the chocolate pieces, stirring briefly. Set aside and allow the warm butter to melt the chocolate. Meanwhile, in the bowl of a stand mixer fitted with a whisk attachment, whip the eggs, sugars, and vanilla extract on high until pale and thick, about 3-4 minutes. Stop the mixer. Add the melted butter/chocolate mixture and whisk on low until incorporated. In a separate bowl, stir together the flour and baking powder. With mixer on low, add the dry ingredients, mixing gently until just incorporated. Stop the mixer, scrape down the sides of the bowl, and continue to beat on low for another 30 seconds. Using a spatula or a wooden spoon, fold in the chocolate pieces by hand. Transfer dough to an airtight container and refrigerate until firm, at least two hours, or overnight.

Preheat oven to 350° F. Line two baking sheets with parchment paper. Using a #80 scoop, shape the cookies into half-rounds. Arrange cookies 2" apart on the baking sheets, staggering each row. Bake until the cookies are just barely beginning to crackle and set - about 8-10 minutes. Do not overbake. You will want these to be set in the middle, but not completely firm. Slide parchment from tray and cool. (Please eat at least one while they are still warm!) Store in an airtight container at room temperature for up to two days.

thumbprint cookies

With an abundance of grey, rainy days here in Oregon, we sometimes need to make a little sunshine of our own. These thumbprint cookies are just the ticket - bright, zesty, and filled with endless possibilities. During the winter months, when citrus is at its peak, we love to fill these with lemon curd. More colorful options include seasonal preserves, such as rhubarb, blackberry, or blueberry.

336 g (1½ c) unsalted butter, softened
finely grated zest of one lemon
14 g (1 T) good quality vanilla extract
560 g (4 c) low-gluten flour
2 g (⅓ t) baking powder

196 g (1 c) granulated sugar
14 g (1 T) lemon juice
47 g (1 large) egg, room temperature
2 g (⅓ t) baking soda
2 g (⅓ t) fine sea salt

filling:

fruit preserves (see page 80) or lemon curd (see page 81)

In the bowl of a stand mixer fitted with a paddle attachment, cream the butter, sugar, and lemon zest until light and fluffy, about 3-4 minutes. Add the lemon juice, vanilla, and egg. Beat on high speed until smooth, another 1-2 minutes. In a separate bowl, stir together the dry ingredients. With the mixer on low speed, add the dry ingredients, mixing gently until evenly incorporated. Scrape down the sides of the bowl and mix another 30 seconds. Cover mixing bowl and transfer to fridge for 30 minutes, or until the dough is just firm enough to scoop. Do not over-chill the dough. This will make it difficult to imprint the cookies.

Preheat oven to 325° F. Using a #80 scoop, shape the cookies into half-rounds. Arrange the pieces 2" apart on parchment-lined sheet pans. With the handle of a wooden spoon dipped in flour, make a deep indent in the top of each cookie. Use your fingers to repair any cracks that have formed. Place desired filling (lemon curd or preserves) in a piping bag fitted with a small (#805) round tip. (Alternately, use a small spoon to fill the cookies.) Fill each indent with a healthy dose of curd or preserves. Bake until the cookies just begin to color at the edges, and filling is bubbly. Slide parchment onto counter or cooling rack. Allow cookies to come to room temperature. Dust with sifted powdered sugar. Store in an airtight container at room temperature for up to four days.

Not a fan of creamy, gooey, or sticky?

Then skip right on by this section.

Because this is all about filling. Sandwich cookies are the touring edition of the baked world - the moonroof of cookies, the power gate of goodness, the 12-speaker sound system of supreme satisfaction. Cookie pieces will get you there, but buttercream and ganache make the ride a blast!

If you are open to experiment, visit the filling and frosting collection on pages 78-83. After all, there's no rule that says lil' mamas have to be filled with vanilla bean buttercream. We love them with mint frosting, bourbon buttercream, and salted caramel buttercream, too.

So please, play with these recipes. Make them your own. Maybe one day you'll want to start your own bakery. Stranger things have been known to happen!

lil' mamas

makes 36 sandwich cookies

One of our all-time favorite employees, Whitney Burnside, arrived at work one day with a burning desire to make a kick-ass chocolate wafer cream cookie. After a few weeks of tweaking and testing, the resulting cookie was deemed a preternatural hit. It never left our menu. Our nickname for the diminutive Whitney was (and still is) "Lil' Mama." How could we call them anything else?

CHOCOLATE WAFERS

224 g (1 c) unsalted butter, softened
112 g (2 jumbo) eggs, room temperature
200 g (2 c) extra dark (22%) cocoa powder
2 g (½ t) baking powder

470 g (2½ c) granulated sugar
280 g (2 c) low-gluten flour
10 g (1¾ t) baking soda
2 g (½ t) fine sea salt

Preheat oven to 325° F. In the bowl of a stand mixer fitted with a paddle attachment, cream the butter and sugar until light and fluffy, about 3-4 minutes. With the mixer on medium speed, add the eggs one at a time, stopping to scrape down the bowl between additions. Beat until fluffy and smooth. In a separate bowl, stir together the dry ingredients. Add to the creamed ingredients, mixing gently until evenly incorporated. Using a #100 scoop, shape the cookies into half-rounds. Arrange the pieces 2" apart on parchment-lined sheet pans. Bake until the cookies just begin to crackle - about 4-5 minutes. Remove tray from the oven briefly and gently flatten each cookie with the bottom of a metal measuring cup. Return to the oven for 2-3 more minutes, until the cookies are just set to the touch. Cool to room temperature before filling.

VANILLA BEAN BUTTERCREAM

224 g (1 c) unsalted butter, softened
seeds from 1/2 vanilla bean
2 g (½ t) salt

210 g (2 c) powdered sugar
10 g (2 t) good quality vanilla extract

In the bowl of a stand mixer fitted with a paddle attachment, cream all ingredients until light and fluffy (about 3-5 minutes on high speed.) Turn ½ of the pieces upside down. Using a piping bag fitted with a round tip (#805) pipe a circle of filling onto each piece. Top with remaining pieces. Chill until set. Store in the refrigerator in an airtight container for up to one week.

passion fruit creams

makes 36 sandwich cookies

Cecelia adapted this recipe from her Australian muse, Donna Hay. If you live in an area with access to fresh passion fruit, your cookies will shine like no other. Be careful not to overbake the pieces - you'll want them to be melt-in-your-mouth soft to accommodate the creamy passion fruit filling.

PASSION FRUIT SHORTBREAD

262 g (18 T) unsalted butter, softened
finely grated zest of one lemon
55 g (⅓ c) fine white rice flour

175 g (1½ c) powdered sugar
315 g (2¼ c) low-gluten flour
56 g (¼ c) passion fruit purée

In the bowl of a stand mixer fitted with a paddle attachment, cream the butter, powdered sugar, and lemon zest until light and fluffy, about 2-3 minutes. With mixer on low, add the two flours, mixing gently until just incorporated (the dough will be a bit crumbly looking at this point). With mixer still running, add the passion fruit purée. Increase speed to medium and beat 30 seconds. Stop the mixer, scrape down the sides of the bowl, and continue to beat at medium for another 30 seconds. Transfer dough to an airtight container and refrigerate until firm, at least 2 hours.

Preheat oven to 350° F. Using a #100 scoop, shape the cookies into half-rounds. Arrange cookies 1" apart on parchment-lined baking trays. Mark each round gently with the tines of a fork. Bake in preheated oven until the edges of the cookies are just beginning to color - about 10-12 minutes. Slide parchment from tray and cool to room temperature.

PASSION FRUIT BUTTERCREAM

125 g (8 T) unsalted butter, softened
56 g (¼ c) passion fruit purée

125 g (1 c) powdered sugar

In the bowl of a stand mixer fitted with a paddle attachment, beat the butter, powdered sugar, and passion fruit purée until light and fluffy (about 5-7 minutes on high speed). Turn ½ of the pieces upside down. Using a piping bag fitted with a round tip (#805), pipe a circle of filling onto each piece. Top with remaining pieces. Dust with powdered sugar and chill until set. Store in the refrigerator in an airtight container for up to one week.

cappuccino creams

makes 48 sandwich cookies

Amazingly, we've been baking these addictive cookies for nearly 30 years. Customers refer to them as the "crack cocaine of cookies." Rumor has it that Elizabeth wooed her husband with a batch of these. The original idea came from an out-of-print British cookbook, and included the addition of dark rum in the filling. We've narrowed it down to one vice, but you can easily fix that with a whiskey back.

ESPRESSO SHORTBREAD

224 g (1 c) unsalted butter, softened
19 g (1 large) egg yolk
14 g (1 T) boiling water

130 g (⅔ c) light brown sugar
9 g (3 T) instant espresso powder
282 g (2 c) low-gluten flour

In the bowl of a stand mixer fitted with a paddle attachment, cream the butter and sugar until light and fluffy, about 3-4 minutes. Add egg yolk, beating until smooth. In a separate bowl, dissolve the espresso powder in boiling water. Add to mixer and beat one minute. Scrape down the sides of the bowl. With mixer on low speed, add the flour, mixing gently until just incorporated. Turn the dough out onto a piece of lightly floured parchment. With floured hands, form the dough into a smooth, round disk. Wrap in parchment and chill for one hour.

Preheat oven to 350° F. On a lightly floured surface, roll dough to an even ⅓" thickness. Cut into 2" circles. Arrange 1" apart on parchment-lined sheet pans. Repeat with remaining dough. Bake cookies until firm to the touch, about 10-12 minutes. Remove from oven. Cool to room temperature before filling.

CINNAMON BUTTERCREAM

210 g (2 c) powdered sugar
1 g (¼ t) fine sea salt
14 g (1 T) good quality vanilla extract

4 g (1½ t) ground Saigon cinnamon
28 g (2 T) unsalted butter, melted
28 g (2 T) heavy cream

Sift dry ingredients into the bowl of a stand mixer fitted with a paddle attachment. With mixer on lowest setting, add the melted butter, vanilla, and cream. Beat on high speed until thick and fluffy. Turn ½ of the pieces upside down. Using a piping bag fitted with a round tip (#805), pipe a circle of filling onto each piece. Top with remaining pieces. Chill until set. Store in the refrigerator in an airtight container for up to two weeks.

cocoa nib stars

makes 36 sandwich cookies

Oh, cocoa nibs. So crunchy, nutty and unusual. We love the texture they add to the simplest recipes. These shortbread-based sandwich cookies have everything a chocolate lover could ever ask for - crunchy cocoa bits, bittersweet chocolate ganache, and a half-dip of even more dark chocolate.

224 g (1 c) unsalted butter, chilled
140 g (⅔ c) granulated sugar
2 g (½ t) fine sea salt
56 g (¼ c) cocoa nibs

280 g (2 c) low-gluten flour
56 g (¼ c) fine, white rice flour
8 g (2 t) ground Saigon cinnamon
one recipe chocolate ganache (see page 83)

Preheat oven to 350° F. Cut chilled butter into ½" cubes. Place all ingredients, including butter, into the bowl of a stand mixer fitted with a paddle attachment. On low speed, mix all ingredients until they become a slightly crumbly, yet cohesive dough (depending on the temperature of your butter, this may take 5-7 minutes.) Turn the dough out onto a piece of lightly floured parchment. Using your hands, bring together the crumbly bits to form a solid disk. Sprinkle with flour and roll to ⅓" thickness. Cut out small stars from the smooth spots. Re-roll remaining dough and repeat. Arrange cookies 1" apart on parchment-lined baking trays. Bake in preheated oven until light golden and firm to the touch, about 10-12 minutes. Remove from oven. Cool to room temperature before filling.

Make ganache as directed. Allow to cool slightly, whisking occasionally, until the mixture is spreadable. Invert half of the shortbread pieces. Transfer the ganache to a piping bag fitted with a round tip (#805). Pipe a generous dot of ganache on each inverted star. Top with remaining pieces. Chill until firm. Half dip each sandwich cookie in tempered chocolate (see page 83). Store in the refrigerator in an airtight container for up to one week.

peanut butter creams

makes 48 sandwich cookies

You know what they say - peanut butter and chocolate are the perfect food. Customers agree, it seems, as these lovelies have achieved a cult-like status. Hats off to Rosie's Bakery, the inspiration for these crunchy, creamy bites of heavenly goodness.

PEANUT BUTTER COOKIES

224 g (1 c) unsalted butter, softened
196 g (1 c) light brown sugar
9 g (2 t) good quality vanilla extract
224 g (1½ c) low-gluten flour
2 g (½ t) baking powder
5 g (1 t) fine sea salt

280 g (1¼ c) creamy peanut butter
196 g (1 c) granulated sugar
94 g (2 large) eggs, room temperature
210 g (2 c) thick cut, whole oats
5 g (1 t) baking soda

In the bowl of a stand mixer fitted with paddle attachment, cream the butter, peanut butter, sugars, and vanilla until light and fluffy, about 3-4 minutes. With the mixer at medium speed, add eggs one at a time, stopping to scrape down the bowl between additions. Beat until fluffy and smooth, 2-3 minutes. In a separate bowl, stir together dry ingredients. With mixer on low, add to the creamed ingredients. Mix gently until incorporated. Transfer to airtight container and chill until firm, at least two hours.

Preheat oven to 350° F. Portion dough using a #100 scoop. Arrange the pieces 2" apart on parchment-lined sheet pans. Bake until the cookies just begin to crack and edges are golden - about 9-10 minutes. Remove tray from oven briefly. Gently flatten each cookie with the bottom of a metal measuring cup. Return to the oven 2-3 more minutes, until the cookies are golden. Cool to room temperature before filling.

PEANUT BUTTER FLUFF

112 g (½ c) unsalted butter, softened
280 g (2 c) powdered sugar

280 g (1¼ c) creamy peanut butter
28 g (2 T) heavy cream

In the bowl of a stand mixer fitted with paddle attachment, cream the butter, peanut butter, and sugar until light and fluffy (about 3-5 minutes on high speed.) Add cream and continue to beat until the mixture is light and spreadable. Turn ½ of the pieces upside down. Using a piping bag fitted with a round tip (#805) pipe a circle of filling onto each piece. Top with remaining pieces. Chill until set. Drizzle with tempered chocolate (see page 83.) Store in refrigerator in an airtight container for up to one week.

lemon ginger creams

makes 36 sandwich cookies

Gingerbread is the odd duck of the baking world. We love to observe the reaction of new bakers when they make gingerbread for the first time, eyes widening in disbelief as the mixture foams up like a blob about to consume the kitchen. One part holiday treat, one part magic - or maybe just a really tasty science experiment.

168 g (⅔ c) blackstrap molasses
10 g (2 t) baking soda
3 g (1 t) ground ginger
1 g (¼ t) ground nutmeg
47 g (1 large) egg, room temperature
2 g (⅓ t) fine sea salt

196 g (1 c) light brown sugar
7 g (2 t) ground Saigon cinnamon
3 g (1 t) ground clove
224 g (1 c) unsalted butter, room temperature
560 g (4 c) low-gluten flour
lemon icing (see page 81)

Combine the molasses and brown sugar in a two quart, stainless steel pot. (This may seem like a large pot for such a small amount of ingredients, but you will need the room.) Over medium heat, bring the mixture to a boil, stirring regularly to avoid scalding. Remove from heat, and carefully add the baking soda all at once. The mixture will begin to bubble and rise. Stir the mixture occasionally as it settles. Transfer to the bowl of a stand mixer fitted with a paddle attachment. Add the butter and dry baking spices. Beat on medium speed until butter melts into the hot mixture. Add the egg and beat until well incorporated. With mixer on low, add the flour and salt, mixing gently until just incorporated. Stop the mixer, scrape down the sides of the bowl, and continue to beat at medium for another 30 seconds. Transfer dough to an airtight container. Refrigerate one hour.

Preheat oven to 350° F. Sprinkle a sheet of parchment with flour. Using a well-floured rolling pin or wooden dowel, roll out the dough to an even ⅓" thickness. Cut out cookies to desired shape. Arrange cookies 1" apart on parchment-lined baking trays. Bake in preheated oven until the edges of the cookies are just beginning to color, the tops are puffy, and the cookies feel set, about 10-12 minutes depending on size. Cool to room temperature before filling.

Prepare lemon icing as directed. Turn ½ of the pieces upside down. Using a piping bag fitted with a round tip (#805) pipe a generous dollop of filling onto each piece. Top with remaining gingerbread pieces. Store at room temperature in a tightly sealed container for up to one week.

hazelnut baci

makes 36 sandwich cookies

In Northern Italy, these "baci di dama," or "ladies' kisses," are a staple at small-town cafes. Throw back a perfectly-made espresso, bite into one of these, and you'll be ready for action. With only five ingredients in the dough, the quality of each item is very important. We suggest you get your hands on some Freddy Guys hazelnuts. Owners Barb and Fritz Foulke take their hazelnuts from catkin to bag right on the farm, including a spin in the grade A nut roaster they imported from Italy.

224 g (1 c) unsalted butter, softened
8 g (1½ t) good quality vanilla extract
chocolate ganache (see page 83)

84 g (⅔ c) powdered sugar
245 g (1¾ c) low-gluten flour
140 g (1⅓ c) ground, roasted hazelnuts

In the bowl of a stand mixer fitted with a paddle attachment, cream the butter, sugar, and vanilla until light and fluffy, about 3-4 minutes. In a separate bowl, stir together the flour and ground hazelnuts. With mixer on low speed, add the dry ingredients, mixing gently until evenly incorporated. Transfer dough to airtight container and chill until firm (about 90 minutes).

Preheat oven to 350° F. Using a #100 scoop, shape the cookies into half-rounds. Arrange the pieces 2" apart on parchment-lined sheet pans. Bake until the cookies are just set and beginning to color at the edges. Remove from oven and cool to room temperature before filling.

Make ganache as directed. Allow to cool slightly, stirring occasionally, until the mixture is spreadable. Invert half of the shortbread pieces. Transfer the ganache to a piping bag fitted with a round tip (#805). Pipe a generous dot of ganache on the flat surface of each cookie. Top with remaining pieces. Roll the edges of each finished baci in ground hazelnuts. Chill until chocolate is set. Store in an airtight container, refrigerated, for up to one week.

carrot cake whoopie pies

We adore carrot cake. But sometimes, you just don't feel like eating a giant piece of cake. These bite-sized whoopie pies deliver all the goodness of fresh carrot cake without the "I'm having a food baby" hangover. For best results, pick up some fresh, sweet carrots from your local farmers' market.

CARROT WHOOPIES

224 g (½ lb) carrots, cooked until soft
94 g (2 large) eggs, room temperature
224 g (1½ c) low-gluten flour
2 g (½ t) ground clove
2 g (½ t) fine sea salt
42 g (¾ c) toasted coconut flakes

197 g (1 c) light brown sugar
112 g (8 T) unsalted butter, melted
3 g (1½ t) ground Saigon cinnamon
2 g (¾ t) ground ginger
5 g (1 t) baking soda

Preheat oven to 350° F. In the bowl of a food processor, purée the carrots and sugar until smooth. With the motor running, add the eggs one at a time, processing one minute after each addition. Add the butter in a steady stream, blending until smooth. In a separate bowl, stir together all remaining ingredients. Add the dry ingredients to the bowl of the processor, pulsing gently until evenly incorporated. Transfer the mixture to a piping bag fitted with a round (#805) tip. Pipe quarter-sized circles, spaced 2" apart, onto parchment-lined sheet pans. Bake the whoopie pies until golden in color and firm to the touch, about 10-12 minutes. Cool to room temperature before filling.

CREAM CHEESE FILLING

184 g (6 T) unsalted butter, softened
9 g (1½ t) good quality vanilla extract
350 g (3 c) powdered sugar

184 g (6 T) cream cheese, softened
finely grated zest of one lemon
2 g (½ t) fine sea salt

In the bowl of a stand mixer fitted with a paddle attachment, cream butter, cream cheese, vanilla, and lemon zest until light and fluffy (about 3-5 minutes on high speed.) Add powdered sugar and salt. Beat until smooth. Turn ½ of the whoopies upside down. Using a piping bag fitted with a round tip (#805) pipe a circle of filling onto each piece. Top with remaining pieces. Chill until set. Store in the refrigerator in an airtight container for up to five days.

raspberry hubba hubbas

What's with the name? If you need to blame someone, Elizabeth's husband, Dan, is the responsible party. Originally called "raspberry creams," Dan deemed the name "not good enough for such an awesome cookie." Once renamed, the moniker stuck. It's fun to say, and even more fun to eat! We often substitute other berries throughout the summer season, changing the hue of this buttercream weekly.

VANILLA BEAN SHORTBREAD

224 g (1 c) unsalted butter, chilled
140 g (⅔ c) granulated sugar
2 g (½ t) fine sea salt

280 g (2 c) low-gluten flour
28 g (2 T) fine, white rice flour
seeds from one vanilla bean pod

Cut chilled butter into ½" cubes. Place all ingredients, including butter, into the bowl of a stand mixer fitted with a paddle attachment. On low speed, mix all ingredients until they become a slightly crumbly, yet cohesive dough (depending on the temperature of your butter, this may take 5-7 minutes). Turn the dough out onto a floured surface. Using your hands, bring together the crumbly bits to form a solid disk. Sprinkle with flour and roll to ⅓" thickness. Cut out small circles from the smooth spots. Re-roll remaining dough and repeat. Arrange cookies 1" apart on parchment-lined baking trays.

Preheat oven to 350° F. Bake in preheated oven until golden at the edges and firm to the touch, about 10-12 minutes. Cool to room temperature before filling.

RASPBERRY BUTTERCREAM

224 g (1 c) unsalted butter, softened
112 g (1/2 c) raspberry preserves (see page 80)
1 g (1/4 t) fine sea salt

224 g (2 c) powdered sugar
5 g (1 t) good quality vanilla extract

In the bowl of a stand mixer fitted with a paddle attachment, cream all ingredients until light and fluffy (about 5 minutes on high speed). Turn ½ of the pieces upside down. Using a piping bag fitted with a round tip (#805) pipe a circle of filling onto each piece. Top with remaining pieces. Chill until set. Store in an airtight container, refrigerated, for up to one week.

marionberry linzer

makes 30 sandwich cookies

Elizabeth learned to bake Linzer from an old Austrian chef back in culinary school. This traditional Viennese pastry can be made with either almonds or hazelnuts. Given our addiction to Freddy Guys hazelnuts, you can guess what we prefer. These cookies are especially pretty in heart-shaped form.

LINZER COOKIES

245 g (1¼ c) low-gluten flour
140 g (1⅓ c) finely ground, roasted hazelnuts
3 g (1 t) ground Saigon cinnamon
finely grated zest of one lemon
8 g (1 t) vanilla extract
47 g (1 large) whole egg

140 g (1¼ c) powdered sugar
7 g (1 T) extra dark cocoa powder
2 g (½ t) baking powder
182 g (13 T) unsalted butter, softened
19 g (1 large) egg yolk

Place all dry ingredients into the work bowl of a stand mixer fitted with a paddle attachment. On low speed, add the butter, mixing until large pieces have disappeared. Add all remaining ingredients. Mix until a soft dough has formed. Turn finished dough out onto a floured piece of parchment. Using floured hands, shape into a smooth disk. Chill until firm, at least 2 hours.

Preheat oven to 350° F. Roll dough to even ¼" thickness. Cut out medium-sized hearts from the dough. Arrange cookies 1" apart on parchment-lined baking trays. Using a smaller heart-shaped cutter, cut a hole in the center of half of the pieces (this will be the frame for the preserves). Re-roll remaining dough and repeat. Bake cookies in preheated oven until firm to the touch, about 10-12 minutes. Cool to room temperature before filling.

FILLING

112 g (½ c) good quality berry preserves (we use preserves made from Oregon Marionberries)

Turn solid heart-shaped cookies upside-down. Spread each with a thick layer of berry preserves. Top with heart-shaped cookie frames. Remove any preserves that have attached themselves to the sides of the cookies. Arrange on a sheet pan and dust with a heavy sifting of powdered sugar. Chill in the refrigerator until set. Store in an airtight container at room temperature for up to four days.

honey grahams

makes 36 cookies

Oh my lord. The smell of these cookies baking is enough to drive you crazy. Your neighbors three doors down may magically appear on your doorstep. Thick cut grahams make a wholesome snack when left to their own devices, but for those who can't resist filling them with fresh marshmallow or drowning them in dark chocolate, we sympathize.

THICK CUT GRAHAMS

227 g (1 c) unsalted butter, softened
85 g (¼ c) raw, local honey
70 g (¾ c) graham flour
2 g (½ t) baking soda
2 g (½ t) mace

50 g (¼ c) light brown sugar
280 g (2 c) low-gluten flour
1 g (¼ t) fine sea salt
8 g (1 T) ground Saigon cinnamon
demerara sugar for finishing

In the bowl of a stand mixer fitted with a paddle attachment, cream the butter, sugar, and honey until light and fluffy, about 3-4 minutes. In a separate bowl, stir together all remaining ingredients. With mixer on low, add the dry ingredients, mixing gently until just incorporated. Stop the mixer, scrape down the sides of the bowl, and continue to beat on low for another 30 seconds. Cover dough and refrigerate 20 minutes.

Preheat oven to 350° F. Line two baking sheets with parchment paper. On a lightly floured surface, roll dough to an even ⅓" thickness. Cut into desired shape. Arrange cookies 1" apart on the baking sheets. Sprinkle each cookie with a pinch of demerara sugar. Bake until evenly golden in color and firm to the touch, 10-12 minutes. Slide parchment from tray and cool. Store in a tightly sealed container at room temperature for up to one week.

At this point, you can choose to fill the grahams with vanilla bean marshmallow (page 82), dip them in tempered dark chocolate (see page 83), or both! Our recipe for marshmallow uses cane syrup, which gives them a molasses-like flavor and faint golden color.

so you want to make
macarons?

macarons
aka: the dominatrix

Oh yes. The heartbreak of many a pastry chef, macarons are a challenge well worth mastering. Entire tomes are dedicated to perfecting the Parisian macaron, but honestly, it's just a matter of practice. So channel your inner Buddah and get cracking!

BASIC ALMOND MACARONS

175 g (1½ c) almond flour
123 g (4 large) egg whites, room temperature
70 g (⅓ c) granulated sugar

280 g (2½ c) powdered sugar
1 g (¼ t) fine sea salt
3 g (½ t) almond extract

Preheat oven to 325° F. Sift the almond flour and powdered sugar into a dry bowl. In the bowl of a stand mixer, warm the egg whites and salt over simmering water, stirring occasionally. Keep the whisk attachment handy. Remove from the heat when egg whites are just warm to the touch. On medium speed, whisk the egg whites until foamy. With mixer running, add the granulated sugar in a steady stream. Increase speed to high. Whip until the meringue forms medium stiff, shiny peaks. By hand, gently fold in the almond mixture and extract. Be sure to incorporate all of the almond mixture evenly, without over mixing. The batter should be thick, not runny.

Transfer batter to a piping bag fitted with a small round (#805) tip. Pipe even, quarter-sized circles onto parchment-lined baking sheets, being sure to leave 1" between each macaron. Carefully lift the filled sheet pan and tap firmly on a countertop 4-6 times, or until the macarons have flattened and lost their point.

Place in oven at uppermost position. When a "pied" has formed (during baking, the batter will separate to form a bottom foot and a rounded top) rotate baking tray to lower rack. Bake until crust is firm, but macarons are still slightly "wiggly." The macarons will have a very slight golden tinge. The goal is to finish with a crunchy exterior but chewy interior. If overbaked, the macaron pieces will be hard and dry. Achieving this texture will take much practice and patience. Cool to room temperature before filling.

Turn ½ of the pieces upside down. Using a piping bag fitted with a round (#805) tip, pipe a small dot of filling onto each piece. See pages (78-83) for filling ideas. Macaron fillings range from thick preserves to buttercream to ganache. Top with remaining pieces. Chill until set. Store in the refrigerator in an airtight container for up to one week.

macaron variations
let the fun begin

BASIL MACARONS

one recipe basic almond macarons   1 oz fresh basil leaves

In the work bowl of a 10-14 c. food processor, grind the granulated sugar and basil into a smooth paste. Warm the egg whites, basil sugar and salt over a double boiler until the sugar has dissolved. Proceed with recipe for basic almond macarons, omitting the almond extract. (As you are progressing, the mixture may take on a brownish-grey color due to oxidation, but don't worry! The macarons will brighten up as they bake.)

ESPRESSO MACARONS

one recipe basic almond macarons   1 T instant espresso powder

Following the instructions for almond macarons, sift the espresso powder with the almond flour and powdered sugar. Proceed with recipe for basic almond macarons, omitting the almond extract.

EARL GREY MACARONS

one recipe basic almond macarons   1 T Earl Grey tea

In the work bowl of a 10-14 c. food processor, grind the Earl Grey tea, almond flour, and powdered sugar until the tea has broken up into a fine powder. Sift as directed. Proceed with recipe for basic almond macarons, omitting the almond extract.

LAVENDER MACARONS

one recipe basic almond macarons   2 T fresh lavender flowers

In the work bowl of a 10-14 c. food processor, grind the lavender, almond flour, and powdered sugar until the flowers have broken up into a fine powder. Sift as directed. Proceed with recipe for basic almond macarons, omitting the almond extract. (Note: do not substitute dried lavender flowers, as these will be much more pungent than the fresh flowers.)

Here's where you'll find all the "non-cookie" cookies.

You know, the ones that have their own category, so to speak. Brownies, lemon bars, tassies, rugelach - varieties that refuse to be categorized. As such, they merit an entire section to themselves.

Once again, we encourage you to play with add-ins, toppings, and flavors. Ramp up your lemon bars by sprinkling a handful of fresh huckleberries on top of the curd. Or maybe put some fresh ginger in the crumble. Brownies, those stalwart, trusty friends, are always up for an exciting twist. Shortbread? Oh, don't get us started. Over the years, we've created more than 50 different flavors of shortbread. Why should you be stuck with just one?

These cookies are just begging for you to come out and play.

crumbly
shortbread

makes 30 cookies

Shortbread is one of the easiest, most versatile cookies we bake. Our recipe includes a measure of rice flour, which gives the finished product a pleasing crumb. Enjoy the buttery base recipe, or step it up by choosing an "add-in" from the list below.

SIMPLE SHORTBREAD

224 g (1 c) unsalted butter, chilled
140 g (⅔ c) granulated sugar
2 g (½ t) fine sea salt

282 g (2 c) low-gluten flour
28 g (2 T) fine, white rice flour
additional flavoring from below, if desired

Cut chilled butter into ½" cubes. Place all ingredients, including butter, into the bowl of a stand mixer fitted with a paddle attachment. On low speed, mix all ingredients until they form a slightly crumbly yet cohesive dough (depending on the temperature of your butter, this may take 3-5 minutes). Turn the dough out onto a piece of floured parchment. Using your hands, bring together the crumbly bits to form a solid disk. Sprinkle with flour and roll to ⅓" thickness. Cut into desired shapes, using the smooth spots. Repeat with remaining dough. Arrange cookies 1" apart on parchment-lined trays.

Preheat oven to 350° F. Bake cookies in preheated oven until light golden and firm to the touch, about 10-12 minutes depending on size. Cool to room temperature. Store in an airtight container at room temperature for up to one week.

ADD-INS

Lemon	finely grated zest of one lemon
Earl Grey	1 T ground Earl Grey tea
Ginger Orange	finely grated zest of one orange, plus ¼ c finely chopped candied ginger
Vanilla Bean	seeds from ½ vanilla bean pod
Maple Sugar	substitute 70 g of maple sugar for 70 g of granulated sugar
Rosemary Pepper	1 T finely minced fresh rosemary, plus ½ t freshly cracked black pepper
Lavender	2 T fresh lavender flowers
Cashew	¼ c chopped, roasted cashews, plus ¼ t cardamom
Matcha	2 T Matcha tea powder

james brownies

Matthew, our friend and customer who laughs like a seal, is a whiz at naming cookies. This might be the only cookie that was named before we even developed a recipe. Just like the "hardest working man in show business," these brownies are sweet, nutty, and full of soul.

BROWNIE BASE

224 g (1 c) unsalted butter, softened
187 g (4 large) whole eggs
7 g (1½ t) good quality vanilla extract
6 g (1 T) extra dark cocoa powder

112 g (4 oz) unsweetened chocolate
392 g (2 c) granulated sugar
140 g (1 c) low-gluten flour
1 g (¼ t) fine sea salt

Melt butter in a small saucepan. Remove from heat and stir in the unsweetened chocolate. Set aside, allowing chocolate pieces to melt. In the bowl of a stand mixer fitted with a whisk attachment, whip the eggs, sugar, and vanilla on high until thick and pale yellow, about 3-4 minutes. Add the chocolate and butter mixture. Mix one minute, or until chocolate is evenly distributed. In a separate bowl, stir together the flour, cocoa powder, and salt. On low speed, add dry ingredients, mixing gently until evenly incorporated. Transfer batter to a 9 x 13-inch glass baking pan lined with parchment. Use an offset spatula to spread the batter evenly.

CHANNELING THE KING OF SOUL

112 g (1 c) bittersweet chocolate pieces

112 g (1 c) roasted hazelnuts, chopped

Preheat oven to 325° F. Sprinkle the chocolate pieces and hazelnuts evenly over the top of the brownie base. Bake until the brownies are firm and puffy, about 25-30 minutes. Remove from oven and cool to room temperature. Cut into 36 even rectangles. Store at room temperature in an airtight container for up to one week.

not-so-thin mint bars

makes 36 bar cookies

How Marven Winters stays so thin is beyond me. One of our favorite farmers, Marven has a well-earned reputation for his unparalleled sweet tooth. As soon as the weather turns chilly, we receive a timely email reminder from Marven titled: MINT BARS. How many does Marven consume each winter? We can't count that high. And our math is good.

one brownie base (see page 63), baked and cooled to room temperature

one batch mint frosting (see below)   tempered chocolate for drizzling (see page 83)

MINT FROSTING

420 g (3¾ c) powdered sugar   56 g (4 T) unsalted butter, melted
4-5 drops essential oil of peppermint (not extract)   ¼ t (1 g) salt
56 g (4 T) heavy cream

In the bowl of a stand mixer fitted with a paddle attachment, cream all ingredients until light and fluffy (about 2-3 minutes on high speed). The frosting should be soft and spreadable.

While the frosting is still soft, spread evenly over cooled brownie base. Refrigerate until firm. Using a thin knife dipped in hot water, cut brownies into 36 even rectangles. Set a wire cooling rack over parchment paper. Arrange the brownies in evenly spaced rows. Dip a fork into tempered chocolate and drizzle over the brownies using an even motion. Cool until chocolate is firm. Store in an airtight container in the refrigerator for up to one week.

chocolate cheesecake brownies

makes 36 brownies

This is pretty much like eating two desserts in one, a totally over-the-top, double chocolate delight. Our chocolate brownie base is swirled with bittersweet chocolate cheesecake filling, creating a textural experience that's out of this world. Be sure not to overbake the brownies, as the cheesecake filling can become dry.

one recipe brownie batter (see page 63)
224 g (1 c) cream cheese
47 g (1 large) whole egg

75 g (⅓ c) dark (60%) chocolate pieces
65 g (⅓ c) granulated sugar
5 g (1 T) dark cocoa powder

Preheat oven to 350° F. Melt the chocolate in a small bowl over simmering water, stirring from time to time. Remove from heat. In the bowl of a stand mixer fitted with a paddle attachment, beat the cream cheese and sugar until smooth. Add the egg. Beat at medium speed until the mixture is a velvety consistency, stopping on occasion to scrape down the sides of the bowl. With the mixer on low, add the melted chocolate in a steady stream, then the cocoa powder. Beat until even in color. Transfer mixture to a piping bag fitted with a small, round tip. Pipe stripes lengthwise over the top of the brownie batter. Using the back of a knife, swirl the cheesecake mixture into the brownie base. Bake 25-30 minutes, or until slightly puffy and set. Remove from the oven and cool completely before cutting. Store at room temperature in an airtight container for up to one week.

lemon crumble bars

A great lemon bar requires two things. 1. Loads of lemon zest 2. Zero cornstarch. Perfect, satiny lemon curd requires that you spend upwards of 15 minutes stirring the egg-heavy mixture over low temperature. There is no easy way out. But oh my goodness, the rewards! Packed with zesty lemon from base to crumble, these lemon bars will light up your world.

224 g (1 c) unsalted butter, chilled
140 g (⅔ c) granulated sugar
2 g (½ t) fine sea salt
one recipe lemon curd (see page 81)

282 g (2 c) low-gluten flour
28 g (2 T) fine, white rice flour
finely grated zest of 2 lemons

Preheat oven to 325° F. Cut chilled butter into ½" cubes. Place all ingredients, including butter, into the bowl of a stand mixer fitted with a paddle attachment. On low speed, mix all ingredients until they form an even, fine crumb (depending on the temperature of your butter, this may take 3-5 minutes).

Evenly sprinkle ⅓ of the lemon crumble into a parchment-lined 9 x 13-inch glass baking pan. Press firmly into the pan so that it forms a smooth base. Bake in preheated oven until the shortbread is light golden in color, about 10-12 minutes. Remove from oven and cool until the pan is no longer hot to the touch.

Spread cooled lemon curd over the shortbread base. Top with an even layer of the remaining crumble. Return to the oven. Bake until the top crumb layer is golden in color and the lemon curd begins to bubble, about 17-20 minutes. Cool to room temperature before cutting. Store in the refrigerator in an airtight container for up to one week.

pecan tassies

Arlean Moser was a peach of a grandmom. Remembered for her endless lists, hand-drawn cards, and musical abilities, she is never far from our hearts, our minds, or our bellies. Although she herself ate like a sparrow, Arlean always had lunch ready for us when we'd visit. At the end of our meal, we'd wait hopefully for these magical, miniature pecan pies to appear.

CREAM CHEESE PASTRY

140 g (1 c) low-gluten flour
84 g (6 T) cream cheese

112 g (8 T) unsalted butter, chilled

Brush the insides of 24 mini-muffin cups with melted butter. Place muffin pans in the refrigerator to chill. In the work bowl of a food processor, pulse the flour and butter until the mixture resembles a coarse meal. Add the cream cheese and pulse until the mixture comes together into a loose ball. Transfer to small bowl for ease of handling.

Using a #70 scoop, portion the dough into 24 equal rounds. Place one round into each of the buttered mini muffin tins. Using a wooden tart tamper or your index finger, press the dough evenly into each tin, working the dough up the sides until it sits 1/8" above the top of the pan. Repair any tears with bits of additional dough. Refrigerate the tart shells while you prepare the filling.

PECAN FILLING

126 g (1 c) roasted pecan pieces
47 g (1 large) whole egg
1 g (¼ t) salt

147 g (¾ c) brown sugar
4 g (1 t) good quality vanilla extract
14 g (1 T) unsalted butter, melted

Preheat oven to 350° F. Place all ingredients in the work bowl of a food processor. Pulse until the mixture comes together, scraping down the work bowl occasionally. Be sure not to over process the nuts into a paste. Using a #100 scoop, fill the tart molds ¾ full. Remove any filling that may have dripped onto the pan in the process. Bake in preheated oven until the edges of the pastry are golden, and the filling is puffy and set. Allow to cool for 15 minutes. Dislodge the tarts by inverting the pan over a piece of parchment, tapping the edge of the pan on the counter if needed. If stuck, use a butter knife to remove the tarts individually. Store at room temperature in an airtight container for up to four days.

seasonal fruit tassies

makes 24 mini tarts

Over the years, Arlean's pecan tassies have taken on a life of their own. The cream cheese pastry being oh-so-flaky and perfect, we often use it to showcase seasonal fruit from local farms. Below, you'll find recipes for a few of our favorites, but don't let that keep you from creating your own.

GINGER PUMPKIN TASSIES

24 miniature tart molds lined with cream cheese pastry (see page 68)

224 g (1 c) roasted fresh pie pumpkin
93 g (2 large) whole eggs
4 g (1 t) freshly grated ginger root
168 g (¾ c) heavy cream

70 g (⅓ c) brown sugar
2 g (1 t) ground Saigon cinnamon
1 g (¼ t) ground clove
chopped, candied ginger (for garnish)

Preheat oven to 350° F. In the work bowl of a food processor, purée the pumpkin and brown sugar until smooth. With motor running, add eggs one at a time. Process 2-3 minutes, until mixture is fluffy. Add baking spices and cream, processing until the mixture is smooth. Transfer to a measuring cup fitted with a spout. Fill each mold to the top of the pastry. Remove any filling that may have dripped onto the pan in the process. Bake until the edges of the pastry are golden, and the filling is puffy and set, about 12-15 minutes. Top each tart with a pinch of candied ginger. Cool 15 minutes. Dislodge the tarts with a butter knife. Store in an airtight container at room temperature for up to four days.

RHUBARB CRUMBLE TASSIES

24 miniature tart molds lined with cream cheese pastry (see page 68)

224 g lemon crumble (see page 67)
98 g (½ c) granulated sugar
4 g (1 t) finely grated orange zest

224 g (2c) fresh rhubarb, finely diced
4 g (1 t) freshly grated ginger root

Preheat oven to 350° F. In a small bowl, stir the rhubarb, sugar, ginger, and orange zest together with a fork. Set aside five minutes. Using a small spoon, fill each mold ¾ full. Top the fruit mixture with a heavy dose of lemon crumble, creating a small dome that rises above each shell. Bake until the edges of the pastry are golden and the filling is bubbling, about 12-15 minutes. Cool 15 minutes. Gently dislodge the tarts with a butter knife. Store in an airtight container at room temperature for up to four days.

pear hazelnut rugelach

makes 48 crescent cookies

Rugelach is an ancient Jewish treat that predates other crescent-shaped pastries, including the croissant. They are most often baked during Hanukkah, but are versatile enough to host an array of seasonal fillings. The flaky cream cheese dough is made without sugar, so it relies upon the filling for its sweetness. Fall fruits and nuts are our favorite go-to ingredients for rugelach.

PEAR BUTTER

448 g (1 lb) ripe pears
seeds from ½ vanilla bean

140 g (½ c) unfiltered honey
finely grated zest of one orange

Peel, core, and roughly chop the pears. In a medium-sized stainless steel saucepan, combine the pears, honey, vanilla bean, and orange zest. Cook over low heat, stirring occasionally, until the pears are soft and have almost dissolved in the liquid. Remove from heat and cool to room temperature. In a food processor or blender fitted with a blade attachment, purée until smooth.

RUGELACH DOUGH

224 g (1 c) unsalted butter, softened
finely grated zest of one lemon
325 g (2¼ c) low-gluten flour

224 g (1 c) cream cheese
14 g (1 T) good quality vanilla extract
280 g (2 c) roasted, finely crushed hazelnuts

In the bowl of a stand mixer fitted with a paddle attachment, cream the butter, cream cheese, lemon zest, and vanilla until smooth. Add the flour, mixing on low speed until the mixture forms a loose dough. Divide into two even pieces. Shape each piece into a smooth disk. Wrap each disk in parchment paper and refrigerate until firm, at least one hour.

Preheat oven to 350° F. Remove one disk from the refrigerator. With a rolling pin and a lightly floured surface, shape the pastry into a circle measuring 14" in diameter. Cover the pastry with a thin layer of pear butter, spreading to within 1" of the edge. Sprinkle ½ of the crushed hazelnuts on top. Use a large knife to cut the circle into 24 even wedges. Starting at the wide end of each triangle, roll into crescent shapes. Place on a parchment-lined baking sheet, 2" apart. Repeat with remaining pastry. Bake until golden, about 20 minutes. Dust with powdered sugar when cool. Store at room temperature in an airtight container for up to four days.

almond anise biscotti

makes 24 biscotti

Biscotti often rank low on the "favorite cookie" scale, and for good reason. The biscotti available at your neighborhood coffee shop have the shelf life of a Twinkie and the personality of a rice cake. Good biscotti should be hard, it's true. After all, these are meant to be dunked in liquid. But dry and flavorless? Not on your life. Our biscotti are dense, chewy, and laden with almond and anise seed.

420 g (3 c) low-gluten or all purpose flour
5 g (1 t) baking powder
8 g (1 T) whole anise seed
48 g (3 large) egg yolks
finely grated zest of one orange

350 g (1¾ c) granulated sugar
5 g (1 t) fine sea salt
94 g (2 large) whole eggs
7 g (1½ t) good quality vanilla extract
168 g (1 c) whole almonds

Preheat oven to 325° F. Place the flour, sugar, baking powder, salt, and anise seed in the bowl of a stand mixer fitted with a paddle attachment. In a separate bowl, lightly whisk the eggs, yolks, vanilla extract, and orange zest. With the mixer on low speed, pour the egg mixture into the dry ingredients. Mix on low until the dough forms large, sticky crumbles. Add the almonds. Continue to mix until the dough comes together in one mass. The entire mixing process may take 5-10 minutes depending on your machine. Go do something nice for yourself while you're waiting. If you stare at it, I swear that dough will never come together.

Turn the dough onto a solid counter or cutting board dusted with flour. Wet your hands slightly with cold water. Form the dough into one even log measuring 16" in length. Place the log diagonally on a parchment-lined sheet pan. Lightly press the log with your hands until it is 1½" thick and 3" wide. Bake until the edges are golden, the top begins to crack, and the log feels firm to the touch, about 40-45 minutes. Remove from oven and cool to room temperature.

Using a sharp, serrated knife, cut the cooled log into 24 even pieces. Lay the cut pieces back on the parchment-lined sheet pan. Return to oven and toast five minutes. Turn each piece over and return to the oven for five additional minutes. Remove from oven and cool. Store in an airtight container at room temperature for up to two weeks.

It's all about the filling.

Meant as a reference section of sorts, the following pages contain recipes for all things gooey, creamy, satiny, and sticky. In essence, everything you might envision as filling.

Seasonal preserves, buttercream, salted caramel, ganache - you name it.

Oh, and ice cream. Because who doesn't crave an ice cream sandwich in the middle of August? If you are dedicated enough to fire up those ovens during the dog days of summer, you definitely deserve to cool yourself down on the flip side.

swiss buttercream

Now that you've perfected those Parisian macarons, let's take this to the next level, shall we? Those tooth-some, chewy meringue pieces are just crying out to be sandwiched together. A tiny dollop of silky, sweet buttercream is just the ticket. With a bit of patience and a general understanding of temperature control, mastery of this versatile filling is easily within reach.

123 g (4 large) clean* egg whites

336 g (1½ c) unsalted butter, softened

130 g (⅔ c) granulated sugar

2 g (½ t) fine sea salt

In the work bowl of a stand mixer, combine the egg whites and sugar. Place over a small pot of sim-mering water. Warm the egg white and sugar mixture, stirring regularly with a whisk to avoid cooking the whites. When sugar has dissolved and the mixture is warm to the touch, remove the bowl from heat. Using the whisk attachment, whip the egg mixture on high speed until it forms thick, glossy peaks. Slow the mixer to medium-low speed. With the mixer running, cut pieces of the soft butter into the meringue. As you do this, the mixture will loosen. After you have fed all of the butter pieces into the mixer, turn the speed up to high. After 3-5 minutes, the mixture will begin to emulsify. At this point, you may add the salt and any additional flavoring. Continue to whip until light and fluffy.

If at any point the mixture begins to look curdled, remove the bowl from the mixer and warm briefly over simmering water before returning to the mixer once again. (This is an indication that your butter was too cold.) Should the mixture appear soupy instead, place the bowl into the refrigerator for a few minutes, then return to the mixer. (This is prone to happen during the summer months, and means your overall mixture was too warm.)

If using buttercream immediately, transfer to a piping bag fitted with a round tip. Store unused but-tercream in an airtight container in the refrigerator for up to 2 weeks. Allow buttercream to return to room temperature and re-whip prior to use.

*clean egg whites are completely free from any bits of yolk

FRESH BASIL BUTTERCREAM

one recipe Swiss buttercream

1 oz fresh basil leaves

In the work bowl of a 10-14 c. food processor, grind the granulated sugar and basil into a smooth paste. Proceed with recipe for Swiss buttercream as instructed.

HONEY BUTTERCREAM

one recipe Swiss buttercream

130 g (½ c) unfiltered honey

Follow instructions for basic Swiss buttercream, omitting sugar and substituting honey in its place. This buttercream must be used within 2-3 days, or it will develop a "cheesy" odor.

CITRUS BUTTERCREAM

one recipe Swiss buttercream

finely grated zest of one lemon, lime, or orange

Follow instructions for basic Swiss buttercream. Add citrus zest when mixture has begun to emulsify.

MOCHA BUTTERCREAM

one recipe Swiss buttercream
1 T espresso powder dissolved in 1 t. hot water

1 oz unsweetened chocolate, melted

Follow instructions for basic Swiss buttercream. Add reconstituted espresso and melted chocolate when mixture has begun to emulsify. This buttercream will be a bit "slippery" in texture.

VANILLA MALT BUTTERCREAM

one recipe Swiss buttercream
seeds from one vanilla bean pod

1 oz (¼ c) malt powder

Follow instructions for basic Swiss buttercream. Add malt powder and vanilla bean as mixture begins to emulsify.

fresh fruit fillings

Simple, pure, and bright, fruit buttercreams and refrigerator preserves are a fabulous way to showcase the seasonal bounty of your back yard or farmer's market. For the preserves, each fruit (or vegetable, in the case of rhubarb) will require a slightly different ratio of produce-to-sugar. Cooking times are dependent on the water content of each fruit, with strawberries requiring the lengthiest cooking time. For added variety, feel free to experiment with spice and citrus additions

SIMPLE FRUIT PRESERVES

RHUBARB

448 g (3 c) fresh rhubarb, roughly chopped

2 pods star anise

196 g (1 c) granulated sugar

finely grated zest of one small orange

RASPBERRY

448 g (4 c) fresh, ripe raspberries

½ vanilla bean, split and seeded

98 g (½ c) granulated sugar

finely grated zest of one small orange

BLACKBERRY

448 g (4 c) fresh, ripe blackberries

½ vanilla bean, split and seeded

130 g (⅔ c) granulated sugar

finely grated zest of one small lemon

Combine all ingredients in a small, stainless steel saucepan. Begin cooking over low heat, stirring occasionally, until the fruit releases enough moisture to melt the sugar. Increase heat to medium. Bring to a simmer and continue to cook another 30 minutes, stirring regularly to prevent scorching. Remove from heat and cool to room temperature. Remove hard flavorings (vanilla bean, star anise, etc.) and transfer to a food processor. Pulse lightly until the larger chunks of fruit have dissolved. Store in an airtight container, refrigerated, for up to one week.

LEMON CURD

140 g (3 large) eggs
294 g (1½ c) granulated sugar
168 g (¾ c) fresh lemon juice

48 g (3 large) egg yolks
finely grated zest of 3 lemons
168 g (12 T) unsalted butter, melted

In a large, stainless steel saucepan, whisk together the eggs, yolks, and sugar. Add the lemon zest and juice. Whisk until sugar lumps have dissolved. Add the butter. Cook on lowest heat setting, stirring constantly with a heat-resistant spatula to prevent scorching. After 10-12 minutes, the mixture will begin to thicken. Continue to stir until the curd reaches 170° F on an instant-read thermometer, or until the curd just begins to bubble. Remove curd from heat. Set a fine mesh strainer over a large glass bowl. Pour the hot curd into the sieve, stirring lightly to encourage settling of the solids. When curd has finished draining, discard the solids. Set curd aside, stirring occasionally until it cools to room temperature. Cover surface with parchment and chill. Finished curd may be stored in an airtight container in the refrigerator for up to two weeks.

LEMON ICING

210 g (2 c) powdered sugar
finely grated zest of one lemon
14 g (1 T) heavy cream

28 g (2 T) unsalted butter, melted
14 g (1 T) lemon juice
1 g (¼ t) fine sea salt

In the bowl of a stand mixer fitted with a paddle attachment, cream all ingredients together until smooth and satiny (the filling should be just soft enough to pipe). Use immediately, or store in an airtight container in the refrigerator for up to two weeks.

BLACKBERRY BUTTERCREAM

224 g (1 c) unsalted butter, softened
7 g (1 t) good quality vanilla extract
112 g (½ c) blackberry preserves (see recipe at left)

224 g (2 c) powdered sugar
1 g (¼ t) fine sea salt

In the bowl of a stand mixer fitted with a paddle attachment, cream all ingredients until the mixture is fluffy, and blackberry preserves have emulsified into the buttercream completely (about 5 minutes on high speed). Use immediately, or store in an airtight container in the refrigerator for up to two weeks. (To reconstitute, allow buttercream to come to room temperature, then rewhip until fluffy.)

sticky stuff

VANILLA BEAN MARSHMALLOW

7 g (one packet) plain gelatin
56 g (¼ c) cane syrup
1 g (¼ t) fine sea salt

84 g (6 T) cold water
130 g (⅔ c) granulated sugar
seeds from ½ vanilla bean pod

Place 3 T cold water in bowl of a stand mixer. Sprinkle gelatin over water. Allow to rest five minutes.

In a small, stainless steel saucepan, heat the remaining water, cane syrup, and sugar over medium heat, stirring occasionally. Boil one minute. Add to the bloomed gelatin. Using a whisk attachment, beat on high speed until the mixture resembles soft marshmallow fluff, about 5 minutes. Don't let it get too thick - the thicker it is, the stickier it will be and the harder it is to pipe.

SALTED CARAMEL SAUCE

196 g (1 c) granulated sugar
196 g (14 T) cold, heavy cream
seeds from one vanilla bean pod

56 g (¼ c) cold water
1 g (¼ t) fine sea salt

In a very clean*, medium-sized stainless steel saucepan, combine the sugar and water. Swirl gently to dissolve any sugar lumps (do not use a utensil to stir the mixture). Bring to boil over medium heat. Increase heat to high, and boil until the mixture begins to color at the edges. Swirl the pan occasionally as the sugar caramelizes. It is important not to use a utensil at any time during this process. When the caramel reaches a deep golden brown (about the color of a toasted almond), remove from heat. Carefully add half of the cold cream. The mixture will bubble and sputter a bit. Return to heat and bring to a boil once again. Allow to boil rapidly for two minutes. Remove from heat and transfer to a clean bowl. Whisk in the remaining cream, salt, and vanilla extract. Cool to room temperature. Store in a tightly sealed jar, refrigerated, for up to two weeks.

*It is imperative that your pan be completely clean. If not, your sugar may crystallize as it cooks.

working with chocolate

Tempering your chocolate before dipping or drizzling allows for a shiny, beautiful finish. It also prevents cocoa butter from rising to the top of the hardened chocolate, causing white streaks known as "bloom." The difference in sheen is worth the effort. You'll look like an expert!

TEMPERED CHOCOLATE

In a clean bowl, melt 224 g (2 c) good quality, 70% chocolate over simmering water. As it is melting, stir the chocolate occasionally with a whisk or heat-resistant spatula. When the chocolate reaches 90° F on your thermometer, remove from heat. Stir chocolate from time to time as you are using it, and check temperature frequently. If the temperature dips below 85° F, reheat the chocolate over simmering water once again, stirring until it reaches 90° F.

EASY CHOCOLATE GANACHE

224 g (2 c) good quality dark chocolate (60%)   168 g (¾ c) heavy cream

Place chocolate in a small bowl. Over simmering water, melt the chocolate until smooth, whisking occasionally. Remove bowl from heat. Add the cold cream in a steady stream, whisking until smooth. Allow to cool slightly, stirring occasionally, until the mixture is spreadable. If you plan to use the ganache immediately, transfer to a piping bag fitted with a round tip. Store any remaining ganache in a sealed container in the refrigerator for up to one week.

custard-style ice cream

makes 1 quart

A great ice cream sandwich is such a treat. After working your way through all of these cookie recipes, store bought ice cream really isn't an option, is it? This rich, lightly sweet, vanilla bean ice cream base is lovely all by itself, but put a scoop between two drop cookies, and you've got a party, Buddy.

168 g (¾ c) whole milk
98g (½ c) granulated sugar
1 vanilla bean, split and seeded

336g (1½ c) heavy cream
80 g (5 large) egg yolks

In a small, stainless steel saucepan, combine the milk, half of the heavy cream, and half of the sugar. Bring to a simmer over low heat, whisking occasionally. Remove from heat. Meanwhile, in a small glass bowl, whisk together the egg yolks and remaining sugar. Gradually add the hot liquid to the egg yolk mixture, whisking continuously as you pour the liquid in a steady stream.

Return the mixture to the saucepan. Warm the custard over low heat, stirring constantly with a clean wooden spoon. When the mixture is thick enough to coat the back of the wooden spoon (170° F). remove from heat. Immediately strain into a clean glass bowl. Cool the custard base in an ice water bath until it reaches room temperature. Whisk in the remaining heavy cream and vanilla bean seeds. Cover and refrigerate at least two hours.

Transfer the chilled custard base into the cannister of your ice cream machine. Following the manufacturer's instructions, freeze until the mixture is thick and creamy. Before transferring to an airtight container, add any additional flavorings (cookie crumbs, low-sugar fruit preserves, salted caramel, lemon curd, etc.) Freeze at least two hours before serving. Custard-style ice cream is best eaten within a week of freezing.

CPSIA information can be obtained at www.ICGtesting.com
Printed in the USA
BVIW12n1514080318
509952BV00007B/1

* 9 7 8 0 6 9 2 8 0 0 9 5 9 *